Library of Congress Cataloging-in-Publication Data

Rose Moore, Pauline. Gabriella and Samantha's New Mom. 1st ed.
Includes About the Author.
ISBN-1 978-1-944636-00-5 (e-book)
ISBN-2 978-1-944636-01-2 (pbk)
ISBN-3 978-1-944636-02-9 (hbk)
1. Juvenile Nonfiction: Family - Orphans and Foster Care
2. Juvenile Nonfiction: Family - Adoption
3. Juvenile Nonfiction: Social Issues - Physical Abuse and Emotional Abuse

This book is based on the author's own foster and adoption story. Some characters' names have been changed in order to preserve their privacy.

Printed in the United States of America

10 9 8 7 6 5 4 3 2 1

Gabriella & Samantha's NEW MOM

by
Pauline Rose Moore

illustrator
Fátima Stamato

editor
Anne Hamilton

RM
PRESS

This book is dedicated:

To every little girl and boy in foster care, who hopes to be adopted.

To every adult foster/adoptee: May you see yourself in these pages. You are fearfully and wonderfully made in God's image, and nothing from your story shall be wasted. You are beautiful. You are loved.

To Duane Moore: You loved me through this nerve-wrecking process. Your tender words of affirmation restored my dignity. You and our sons, Elijah & Isaac, believed in me and are three of the best gifts I have ever received. Thank you.

To my biological siblings: Norm, Matt, Jus, Gabe, Mimi, and Dani...it is time to tell your story.

To Joan S. and Barrington S.: You did your best with the tools you had to raise us. It wasn't perfect, but I am grateful because Mom, you didn't have to say, "Yes" to adopting us. You both have played a major part in the Woman of God I am.

To Milton S. (deceased) and Anna S.: Through your union, I was conceived. Our journey to forgiveness was worth it.

To Anne Carson: Before Court Appointed Special Advocates (CASA), you were there. I highly doubt there are many foster moms like you, who would choose to stay and remain an integral part of their past foster child's family...28 years later! You have always been there and you will always be my Godmom.

To CASA: Your continued dedication to help foster children find good homes is unmatched. May God continue to provide you with the volunteers and financial resources needed to sustain CASA in the many years to come.

To Alexis Goring: You are an incredible writer and author. You were the first to offer me a writing gig. You believed in my writing, before I believed it myself. I am thankful for your life.

To Mrs. Baillargeon: You were my voice when I couldn't speak out for myself. You were the best Biology Teacher Hills East ever had, and one of my favorite HS teachers! I am so grateful for you!

To my Church Family: Thank you to my RPC village and every congregation, whose members graciously loved on my family and I. Your prayers are felt wherever I go.

To my Howard University School of Divinity Family and Sorors and Brothers of Kappa Epsilon Psi, Military Sorority, Inc. & Kappa Lambda Chi, Military Fraternity, Inc: The sorority & fraternity sisterhood & brotherhood you give is 2nd to None!

To Darren Cumberbatch: You sharpen me. You are one of the best Graphic Designers I know! Thank you for giving me a taste of my vision made plain. YOU are AWESOMEMINISTRY.ORG!

To Dr. Michael Ingram (DC Poetry Project) and Dr. Jeanette Bryson (Washington Adventist University): Your encouraging words spoke life into my book's future.

Your prayers were what I needed!

Thank you for " unofficially" editing the final draft!

To Anne Hamilton (Editor) and Fatima Stamato (Illustrator): I could not have done this without you. You were both divinely appointed to me and I am grateful for your diligence & expertise.

Thank you for helping me make "it" plain.

To my Friends, Mentors, and Coaches: God allowed our paths to cross for such a time as now. You have poured in and over me with intercessory prayers (some for years), weekly text, social media, & email check-ins just to encourage me. I am grateful for your love. Thank you!

"Will she like me?" Samantha slipped her hand inside her sister's.

"Will she like **us**?" Her eyes were blurring. "Goodbye, city." She pressed her face against the warm glass to hide her tears. The city shrank far too quickly. Soon the tall buildings were midgets, but the fears inside her were growing like giants.

"Will she let us room together?"

"You'll soon see," Amy, the social worker, said.

Samantha watched her sister closely. *Is she **afraid?*** Samantha wondered. She noticed Gabriella's eyebrows do a funny furrow dance just like hers, when she is deep in thought. She stared as Gabriella rubbed her sweaty palms on her pants. *She is scared,* Samantha realized. "At least we will still be together."

Samantha exhaled, hoping to ease her sister's worry. Samantha squeezed her eyes shut. She shuddered at the thought of being placed in another separate foster home. *My first foster family was mean to me,* she remembered. She didn't want to be alone again and didn't like seeing Gabriella this way.

Gabriella let out a deep sigh. She reached for her orange teddy bear on the seat beside her and squeezed its left leg. It made her feel **safe**.

This will be our third foster home, she thought.

She watched Amy as she drove along the busy highway.

What has Amy told our new mom?

That I still wet the bed?

That I need help to read?

That bad things happened to me when I was a little girl?

That it didn't work out the last two times?

Gabriella's stomach began to fill with butterflies. Amy wasn't telling them anything. The butterflies reminded her of the last time she saw her birthparents in the courtroom with her brothers and sister. Her heart sank. She really missed them.

Why did my parents have to do drugs?

Why did the state have to take us away?

*Why couldn't I stay with my **real** family?*

She thought about her first foster mom, Anne. *She was **nice to me**.* Suddenly, Gabriella grew sad. She remembered the day when she was in Anne's little apartment when the phone rang; she heard Samantha screaming and crying on the phone, because she said her foster parents beat her with a belt. She said her foster sister didn't like her and told them that she ate a mothball when it wasn't true. She said her foster parents beat her whenever they were angry. *She didn't do anything.* Gabriella shook her head desperately trying to blot out the memory. *I am glad we are together **again**.* She folded her arms. *Why can't we go and live with Anne?*

She had been taken from Anne as soon as she started talking about adopting her. All because she was single — and had a different skin color.

Why do such things matter so much?

*Why are such things more important than **love**?*

Samantha and Gabriella leaned forward as Amy slowed on an exit ramp. **"Look!"** Gabriella exclaimed. As the car sped around the curb, Gabriella slipped out of her seatbelt and moved to Samantha's window. Her dark brown eyes grew wider and wider. She had never seen so much greenery in her life! *It's **beautiful**, she thought.*

"What's our new mom like?"

Will she want us to do lots of chores? Samantha asked.

"You'll soon see," Amy said.

"What's our new school like?"

Will there be lots of homework? Samantha asked.

"You'll soon see," Amy said.

"Are there other foster kids there?"

Will they like us or fight us? Gabriella asked.

"You'll soon see," Amy said.

Gabriella twisted her mouth. It really annoyed her when Amy repeated, "You'll soon see." *I hope there aren't any other foster kids at the **new house**.*

She wanted a mom that wasn't too busy to take time to get to know her. That was the reason they had to leave their last foster home.

Mom McDaniels was caring, yet there were so many kids in her care, she couldn't cope; even with her husband's help. Samantha loved it because they'd roomed together there, but Gabriella wanted a space of her own.

Gabriella stared at the grass as they headed into the suburbs. It wasn't a few weeds sprouting from the concrete in an abandoned block. It was a wide, wide, wide living carpet of the brightest **green**. There wasn't a sidewalk in sight.

"Where will we ride our bikes?"

"You'll soon see," Amy said.

Samantha was surprised when the car stopped. "We're here! We're here!" The fear giants inside had disappeared, blown away by a rising bubble of excitement. She jumped out of the car and took in the blue house with its garden of flowers.

*It looks **friendly** enough.* A long driveway was shaded by two tall trees. *We can ride our bikes there!* She skipped up the path to the door and rang the bell.

Gabriella got up on her knees and peered out the car window. She was curious, but she was much too anxious to see who would come to the door. She bit her fingers nervously.

*Will she **like** me?*
*Will she look like **me**?*

The door opened and a woman with the biggest smile swept Samantha into her **arms**.

Gabriella watched their embrace from the car and noticed a small grey cat with blue eyes. *Oh, Sammy's going to love having a cat!* She wasn't so sure herself.

"Are you going to meet your new mom?" Amy asked.

Gabriella didn't move. She couldn't. She felt **stuck**. She couldn't bear the thought of having her hopes built up, only to be disappointed again. She didn't want another mom to take her in, only to let her go when it didn't work out.

The woman walked to the car, hand in hand with Samantha. Her face was grave. "Hello Gabriella." Her voice was soft, like Anne's. "Will you **please** come out?" Gabriella hopped out of the car, her eyes on her own feet all the time.

"Gabriella?" She gently lifted Gabriella's chin and said, "I know when you look at me you see someone who does not look like you, talk like you, or know, you." Her sudden smile was all sunshine and summer joy. "But **I love you** and Samantha already, as if I had had you **myself**."

She laughed as she wrapped Gabriella and Samantha in a warm hug. "**Welcome home**, little daughters."

About the Author

Pauline Rose Moore, MA, was born in Brooklyn, NY and currently lives in Bowie, MD, with her husband and two sons. Pauline is passionate about children in foster care and adoption, and gives annually to Court Appointed Special Advocates (CASA), in their efforts to help every abused or neglected child in the U.S., find a safe and permanent home, where he/she can thrive. Pauline shares pieces of her own foster and adoption story, through Gabriella's eyes, in an effort to help fosters and adoptees (adults too) find encouragement and have hope restored. Pauline is a proud Air Force Reserve Servicemember & Veteran, American Sign Language Interpreter & and Class of 2017, Howard University School of Divinity degree Candidate, where she is pursuing her calling to ministry as the first Seventh-Day Adventist Chaplain on active duty, in the United States Air Force.

Did you enjoy the book? Pauline would like to hear from you!

Please connect with her to share your thoughts, and be one of the first to be notified about upcoming projects and learn what Gabriella & Samantha are up to next!

You may connect with her via:

social media @ Pauline Rose Moore
email: paulinerosemoore@gmail.com
www.paulinerosemoore.com

Thank you for purchasing and/or taking the time to read her book!

CPSIA information can be obtained
at www.ICGtesting.com
Printed in the USA
BVHW020204180821
614683BV00017B/808

9 781944 636029